MW01107601

Lawrence & Holloman

Morris Panych

Talonbooks
1998

Copyright © 1998 Morris Panych
Published with the assistance of the Canada Council.

Talonbooks
#104—3100 Production Way
Burnaby, British Columbia, Canada V5A 4R4

Typeset in New Baskerville and Frutiger and printed and bound in
Canada by Hignell Printing.

First Printing: August 1998

Talonbooks are distributed in Canada by General Distribution Services,
325 Humber College Blvd., Toronto, Ontario, Canada M9W 7C3;
Tel.: (416) 213-1919; Fax: (416) 213-1917.

Talonbooks are distributed in the U.S.A. by General Distribution
Services Inc., 85 Rock River Drive, Suite 202, Buffalo, New York, U.S.A.
14207-2170; Tel.: 1-800-805-1083; Fax: 1-800-481-6207.

Canadian Cataloguing in Publication Data

Panych, Morris.
    Lawrence & Holloman

    A play.
    ISBN 0-88922-392-0

    I. Title.   II. Title: Lawrence and Holloman.
PS8581.A65L38 1998   C812'.54   C98-910723-X
PR9199.3.P325L38 1998

Lawrence & Holloman was first produced at the Tarragon Theatre in Toronto on April 28, 1998 with the following cast:

LAWRENCE   Richard Zeppieri

HOLLOMAN   Richard Waugh

Directed by Morris Panych
Set & Costumes designed by Ken MacDonald
Lighting designed by Bonnie Beecher
Original Music & Sound Design by Jeff Corness
Stage Manager Winston Morgan

1. Beer and befriending

*Drinking beer. Two gentlemen sit together close enough that
LAWRENCE, the younger, handsomer, and more self-possessed of
the pair—has his arm draped around HOLLOMAN, his bug-like
companion. LAWRENCE, eyes wide with anticipation, waits for
HOLLOMAN's reaction.*

HOLLOMAN
    A future?

LAWRENCE
    A *future.*

HOLLOMAN
    What does that mean?

LAWRENCE
    You're such a neurotic, *Harmon*—such a—

HOLLOMAN
    Holloman.

LAWRENCE
    What does it *mean?* Come here!

Pulling him closer.

HOLLOMAN
    Please.

LAWRENCE
    It's as simple as this. He's trying to tell me that I'm
    going places in the department. See? Advancing up the
    ladder. Up. The ladder. Like that game. That—you
    know?

HOLLOMAN
   No.

LAWRENCE
   With the snakes. The snakes.

HOLLOMAN
   I don't—

LAWRENCE
   Sure you do. When you were a kid. With the dice.

HOLLOMAN
   I can't imagine somebody having a future.

LAWRENCE
   It's because you're in shoe sales.

HOLLOMAN
   What gave you that idea?

LAWRENCE
   You are so cute. "I can't imagine...."

HOLLOMAN
   You're—choking me.

LAWRENCE
   God, I feel good, Harmon. Look at me. Look how good
   I feel.

HOLLOMAN
   You must be on top of the world right about now.

LAWRENCE
   You know what? I could eat the world with a spoon. A
   spoon.

HOLLOMAN
From the men's wear department, who knows where
you could go.

LAWRENCE
Let's have another beer.

HOLLOMAN
Please.

LAWRENCE
Sorry.

HOLLOMAN
So what are your—personal plans? Your—

LAWRENCE
My—?

HOLLOMAN
You know.

LAWRENCE
Personal?

HOLLOMAN
Concerning, you know, your fiancée and all that. You
said you were engaged?

LAWRENCE
I don't follow you, Harmon.

HOLLOMAN
Will you get married now? I guess you'll get married
now.

LAWRENCE
    I suppose I could. I suppose that would be the—

HOLLOMAN
    —logical...

LAWRENCE
    —thing. The...right. The...

HOLLOMAN
    ...inevitable....

LAWRENCE
    Now that I'm advancing up the—

HOLLOMAN
    Right.

LAWRENCE
    Now that my future is—hey. Let's not talk about this.
    No, no let's. You're right, Harmon. You're absolutely—
    as usual, you're—I should get married, shouldn't I?
    Settle down and all that—you know—that—

HOLLOMAN
    —that—?

LAWRENCE
    It's just, the thing is, I mean—what about all those
    other women who are still in love with me? I don't
    mean to—you know. But it's true. Not to mention the
    ones I haven't even met, yet. I mean—

HOLLOMAN
    The legions of broken-hearted?

LAWRENCE

I mean—the what? To hell with it, Harmon. You're
right. I'm going to do it. To hell with it. I'm going to get
married. God damn it, I am going to get married. Let's
have another beer. Let's have a whole lot more beer.
We're going to drink tonight, Harmon. And then we're
going to go out on the town. You know what I mean by
out on the town, don't you? I mean—out. On the town.

HOLLOMAN

Oh, I—

LAWRENCE

Hey. Harmon. Stop thinking like a shoe salesman. You
think like a shoe salesman.

HOLLOMAN

I'm not—I'm—

LAWRENCE

Exactly. What?

HOLLOMAN

—not.

LAWRENCE

I know so little about you, Harmon. So little. Isn't that
strange?

HOLLOMAN

Not really. We only just —

LAWRENCE

Just what, Harmon?

HOLLOMAN

Met.

LAWRENCE
Did we? Jesus. You're right. We only just met.

HOLLOMAN
And it's Holloman.

LAWRENCE
What is?

HOLLOMAN
My name. It's Holloman.

LAWRENCE
You know what? You should grow a moustache. It
would—it would—I don't know—what am I trying
to say?

HOLLOMAN
I don't know. What are you trying to say?

LAWRENCE
Hide your face a little. Divert attention.

HOLLOMAN
Yes. That would be—

LAWRENCE
Frankly, you could use a little more.... Are you listening
to me? Harmon? Are you paying attention?
Pay attention! I'm telling you something here.

HOLLOMAN
You keep calling me Harmon. I don't know why. If you
want to keep calling me Harmon, that's fine. But it's
Holloman. Actually.

Beat.

10

LAWRENCE
Wow. You're pretty particular, aren't you?

HOLLOMAN
Yes.

LAWRENCE
Yes. But then, you like to stay on top of things. You, like, to be, precise. Yes. Sir. That's my old buddy *Holloman.* Am I right? Am I right? Always on top of things? Come here! Hey *Holloman.*

HOLLOMAN
Yes?

LAWRENCE
Try not to be too particular. It's not the best way to make a new friend.

HOLLOMAN
Right.

LAWRENCE
Now go get me a beer.

Music. Blackout

2. If the shoe fits

Some days later. A park. HOLLOMAN and LAWRENCE with brown bag lunches.

LAWRENCE
　White bread and baloney?

HOLLOMAN
　Maybe.

LAWRENCE
　Not maybe. You are a white bread and baloney type of guy. I mean—Holloman. Look at you. Have you ever thought of doing anything unpredictable? Ever?

HOLLOMAN
　You mean—like...mustard?

LAWRENCE
　With your life, Holloman. Your *life.* Just right off the top of your head? Just a spur of the moment—

HOLLOMAN
　My life is....

LAWRENCE
　Exactly. Is what? Hey, Holloman. Do I look happy? Tell me. Do I look happy? What do I look like? Tell me what I look like.

HOLLOMAN
　Happy?

LAWRENCE

Holloman, I am happy. I am a happy man. A happy, happy man. It's a funny word, happy—isn't it? If you say it enough it doesn't sound happy at all.

HOLLOMAN

Not especially, no.

LAWRENCE

Happy? [*Sadly*] Happy. [*Cheering*] I'm joyous, Holloman. Joyous.

HOLLOMAN

So when's the joyous day?

LAWRENCE

The what? I don't know. We didn't really set a date. Did we? I can't remember. We must have. What difference does it make? Details. There you go. What did I tell you about details, Holloman? You need to relax a little. You have your prostate to consider. June fifth, or something. Her family has millions. That's the important part. Did I ever tell you how much money they have? Do you have any idea how much?

HOLLOMAN

Millions?

LAWRENCE

No. But a lot of money.

HOLLOMAN

Things just fall your way, don't they?

LAWRENCE

They do, don't they? Things really do just fall my way. It's true. I just have to look around sometimes and realize. My mother used to say 'just take a look around you.' But then she got hit by that—bus. But you know what I'm saying. You have to look around. Compare your life to somebody else's. I mean, look at that old drunk over there. That drunk. There. In the hat. Wow.

They look at him.

When you reach the end of the line, Holloman, that's what happens. They give you that hat.

HOLLOMAN
I think he has some kind of palsy.

LAWRENCE
What? Him? Really? No.

HOLLOMAN
He always comes here. He has some kind of palsy.

LAWRENCE
That's beside the point. You wouldn't want to have *palsy*, either. Or would you? Sometimes I wonder, Holloman. You're such a—you're such a—an *unusual* person. The point is—

HOLLOMAN
No. I wouldn't.

LAWRENCE
—the point is—what is the point? Jesus, you've made me lose my thread here.

HOLLOMAN
You were feeling sorry for that man.

LAWRENCE

Holloman, please. You get what you get in this life. If you went around feeling sorry for people, you'd have to feel sorry for just about everybody. I suppose you do. Mr. Liberal. Mr. 'I feel sorry for everybody.'

HOLLOMAN

Where do you get that?

LAWRENCE

Exactly. And do you know why you feel sorry for them? Because you emphasize with them.

HOLLOMAN

Emphasize?

LAWRENCE

It means you identify. You identify with losers.

HOLLOMAN

No I don't.

LAWRENCE

Don't say you don't. I know you, Holloman.

HOLLOMAN

We only met two days ago.

LAWRENCE

Details. Jesus. I don't have to know someone to know them. I just. Know them.

HOLLOMAN

I see.

LAWRENCE

You're such a liberal, Holloman. It makes me laugh.

Actually, it doesn't make me laugh. I'm not sure what it makes me do. It makes me shake my head. Look. [*Shaking his head*] A liberal.

HOLLOMAN
I'm not. At all.

LAWRENCE
I mean, sure—of course. People without legs, I suppose. Or noses. Now there's—I saw a lady without a nose, once. In a smoked-meat restaurant. Why would you have to have your nose removed? What on earth could be so bad about your nose that you'd actually have to have it physically removed? It put me right off my corned beef, you know. I couldn't help thinking her nose was in my sandwich, right? Oh, and I shook a guy's hand, once. He only had two fingers. The rest was melted off. But I didn't feel sorry for him. Why should I? He's making his way in this world. And hey. He's got a thumb. A thumb. These guys—the ones that are making their way in the world. They don't want you to feel sorry for them.

HOLLOMAN
I don't.

LAWRENCE
[*On a serious note*] You know who I'd feel sorry for? A guy without a penis.

HOLLOMAN
Do you know any?

LAWRENCE
Where would I meet a guy without a penis? Jesus. I'm just saying. If you didn't have a penis, that would be— for a guy—that would be bad.

HOLLOMAN

I would think...especially for a—guy.

LAWRENCE

Or a really small penis, I suppose. That would be just about as bad. Oh. Sorry. I didn't mean to—sorry.

HOLLOMAN

What?

LAWRENCE

What?

HOLLOMAN

I'm not...really following the direction of this conversation at all.

LAWRENCE

We were talking about our lot. In life, Holloman. Our lot.

HOLLOMAN

I see.

LAWRENCE

For example, this guy I saw, wandering around in broad daylight, wearing house slippers. House slippers with plastic cling wrap inside, right? He's going through the garbage and he pulls out a cup of coffee that someone else didn't finish drinking. He opens up the lid. He drinks it. Know what I mean?

HOLLOMAN

Not—really.

LAWRENCE

The guy is showing some initiative, Holloman.

You don't need to feel sorry for him.

HOLLOMAN
   Even if he didn't have a penis?

LAWRENCE
   Why wouldn't he?

HOLLOMAN
   I don't know.

LAWRENCE
   Jesus. Holloman. Besides, he can always go out and get
   a job. If he wants.

HOLLOMAN
   What if there aren't any?

LAWRENCE
   You're so cute. You're such a cute little liberal. Look at
   you. "What if there *aren't* any?"

HOLLOMAN
   I read somewhere...

LAWRENCE
   Read somewhere! O.K.

HOLLOMAN
   I read somewhere that it's necessary to the economy—

LAWRENCE
   The economy, right. The economy. Yes, yes. Go on. I'm
   listening. I'm listening. Hey. Holloman. Look. I'm
   listening.

HOLLOMAN
It's necessary—that—that there be a certain percentage of unemployed at any given time. In order for the economy to—to—

LAWRENCE
This is very informative.

HOLLOMAN
In order for some to succeed, some have to fail.

LAWRENCE
Is that so? Who told you that? Some liberal friend of yours. Some big old lesbian.

HOLLOMAN
I read it.

LAWRENCE
Uh, huh. Let me ask you something. Can I ask you something?

HOLLOMAN
What?

LAWRENCE
Are you unemployed? Tell me: are—you—unemployed?

HOLLOMAN
No.

LAWRENCE
Am I?

HOLLOMAN
No.

LAWRENCE

Holloman. I rest my case. I know it's unpopular for me to say this, but a lot of these guys don't even want to work. They don't want to. Let me tell you a story, and I think this will illustrate things a little more clearly for you. About the way the economy works, etc. There was this chicken, right? This hen. And she wanted to make some bread. A nice loaf of bread. Right?

HOLLOMAN

Chickens can't make bread.

LAWRENCE

What?

HOLLOMAN

I've never heard of a chicken that could make bread.

LAWRENCE

This one could. She was a special kind of chicken that could make bread.

HOLLOMAN

What kind of bread, exactly?

LAWRENCE

Relax. It's a story, Holloman. A story.

HOLLOMAN

I'm only—

LAWRENCE

White bread, O.K.? White bread, with little sesame seeds, and sunflower seeds and Jesus anyway—there's this hen. And she goes around asking all the other farm animals—pigs and ducks and so on—to help her make this bread. Right?

HOLLOMAN
But nobody helps her make it.

LAWRENCE
That's right.

HOLLOMAN
So she won't let them eat any of it when she's finished.

LAWRENCE
You know this story?

HOLLOMAN
I think we read it in grade two.

LAWRENCE
Yeah? I'm not surprised we read it in grade two. It's a good story. It beautifully and simply illustrates a point. Everybody has to pitch in and do their share. That's the moral. Of the story. See?

HOLLOMAN
Why?

LAWRENCE
What?

HOLLOMAN
Why should we pitch in and do our share? What do we get out of it?

LAWRENCE
A slice of bread, Holloman.

Beat.

You know, you're a nice guy, but you're incredibly naïve.

Beat.

I want you to come to my stag party. We'll probably be
hiring a woman to have sex with a dog or something.
Shoot ping pong balls out of her snatch. It'll be an
education for you.

HOLLOMAN
I think I'm busy that night.

LAWRENCE
What is it, exactly, that you've got against women?

HOLLOMAN
Me? Nothing.

LAWRENCE
Then why don't you ever want to go out on the town?

HOLLOMAN
I don't know.

LAWRENCE
Are you sure you're not a homosexual? You could be a
homosexual, you know. Just a sad, sad, skinny little
homosexual. A guy your age is just too old to be living
with his mother.

HOLLOMAN
I don't live with my—mother. I—

LAWRENCE
You're peculiar, aren't you? An *oddity*, I'd have to say.

HOLLOMAN
Not—really.

LAWRENCE
Well, I'd have to say you are, Holloman. An *oddity*.
We've got to get you laid. We can't have you going
around not having sex, ever.

HOLLOMAN
What makes you think I don't have sex?

LAWRENCE
Holloman. Please. Maybe by accident.

HOLLOMAN
I—I have—I—I have—I—

LAWRENCE
That is a perishable item you got down there. You have
to use it before a certain expiration date.

Beat.

Did your mother make you that lunch? Here. Trade me
lunches.

HOLLOMAN
Why?

LAWRENCE
It's an exercise. You need to take a few risks in your life.
Risks. Happiness is anticipation, Holloman.
Anticipation.

HOLLOMAN
What about the consequences?

LAWRENCE
Fine. O.K.

Taking out his lunch.

> But Holloman. If you accept things the way they are,
> then that's the way they'll always be. White bread.
> Baloney.

*LAWRENCE crumples and tosses the bag away and walks off
eating a sandwich. HOLLOMAN opens his lunch bag. Carefully
removes his sandwich, places it on his lap. Opens it. Studies it.
This isn't his lunch.*

Blackout.

3. What lunch hath wrought

Staff lunchroom. Days later.

LAWRENCE
Holloman! Go ahead. Congratulate me, Holloman.

HOLLOMAN
Congratulations.

LAWRENCE
You don't know, do you? Jesus. I can't believe how
slowly word travels down to that shoe department.

HOLLOMAN
I told you I don't—

LAWRENCE
So there's been no official announcement of any kind.
Great.

HOLLOMAN
Sorry. No.

LAWRENCE
That's just great. That's terrific. I set the sales record
for March. That's all. The sales record. For March.
That's two months in a row. Two—months—in—a row.
Who's ever done that before? Can you tell me who's
ever done that before?

HOLLOMAN
No one?

LAWRENCE
Absolutely—I'll tell you who. Absolutely no one.

HOLLOMAN
That's amazing.

LAWRENCE
Yes. And you know what I think accounts for it?
I don't want to blow my own horn here.

HOLLOMAN
No. Go ahead.

LAWRENCE
Well, I think part of it's my charm, certainly. But I
think a lot of it has to do with my understanding of
people. My *acumen*. Don't worry, I looked it up.
It's not one of those words I carry around in my head
all the time. But I was trying to define myself the other
night. I just was standing there in the mirror, and I was,
well, you know, studying myself, the way you do, and I
was thinking 'how would I best describe me?' How
would I define this person. That's when I found
acumen in the dictionary.

HOLLOMAN
You have a dictionary?

LAWRENCE
It means keen insight.

HOLLOMAN
Really?

LAWRENCE
You don't have much of an appetite, do you?

HOLLOMAN
  Me?

LAWRENCE
  Do you know where it comes from, I think?

HOLLOMAN
  Gastritis?

LAWRENCE
  What? What are you talking about?

HOLLOMAN
  Sorry. What...?

LAWRENCE
  We were talking about my keen insight. My prescience.
  My grandfather was a water-witcher. He could take an
  ordinary—I'm not kidding—I think it was a willow
  branch—and find water in the ground. My talent is
  different, of course. Some guy walks in, I can tell you
  what kind of suit he's going to walk out with.

HOLLOMAN
  How?

LAWRENCE
  Good question. It's my acumen. You can't explain that
  kind of talent, Holloman. Some people have it. Some
  people don't.

HOLLOMAN
  Why, I wonder?

LAWRENCE
  Why what?

HOLLOMAN
How is it that some people can have so much going for them and other people not have anything going for them at all?

LAWRENCE
Is that what this is? Listen to me. Forget about the other night, would you? That woman just wasn't your type.

HOLLOMAN
She was pretty old.

LAWRENCE
I think they're a mother/daughter team. Forget it. It doesn't make you any less of a person. You're just lacking a spark. Some people just lack a spark.

HOLLOMAN
Why is that? Why do some people lack a spark?

LAWRENCE
I've asked myself that very question. Because it doesn't seem fair, does it? You know what I think it is? Destiny.

HOLLOMAN
Is that it?

LAWRENCE
That's it. Everyone has a purpose. But some have a greater purpose. It's like ants. They all work, they're all workers, right—but one of those ants is called the drone, and his destiny is to have sex with the queen.

HOLLOMAN
Unless you step on him.

LAWRENCE
Why would you step on him?

HOLLOMAN
I don't know. Haven't you ever stepped on an ant before? It seems to me that would...change his destiny.

LAWRENCE
His destiny is to get laid, Holloman. That's his God-given destiny.

HOLLOMAN
You're a religious man, then?

LAWRENCE
No. Jesus. Why? Are you? Tell me you're not.

HOLLOMAN
There are parts of the Bible I find entertaining.

LAWRENCE
Oh, sure. Parts.

HOLLOMAN
Floods and so on.

LAWRENCE
But you're not—?

HOLLOMAN
Not particularly.

LAWRENCE
God was invented by a bunch a losers. You know that don't you?

HOLLOMAN

I thought, perhaps, he was the expression of our better
nature.

LAWRENCE

Our what? Our, please, our—better nature? Listen.
When you see—on T.V.—one of those—you know—
those wild animal kingdom shows, where some great
big snake's got some cute little hamster half-way down
his throat. You tell me. What expression of nature is
that? If there was a God, Holloman, trust me, the
hamster would eat the snake. So please. Religion?
Exactly.

HOLLOMAN

Right.

LAWRENCE

Isn't it bad enough I have to get married in a church
now?

HOLLOMAN

You're getting married in a church?

LAWRENCE

Are you kidding? A cathedral, she wants to get married
in. Like the Princess of—you know—whatever. But I
had to say yes, in the end. Last night I finally had to say
'yes.' I relented, Holloman.

HOLLOMAN

You?

LAWRENCE

We had a little spat, I guess you could call it. So I
relented, yes.

HOLLOMAN
Really.

LAWRENCE
You always have to appear flexible in a relationship, Holloman. Especially when you're on the losing end of the argument.

HOLLOMAN
You had a fight?

LAWRENCE
Not a fight. An argument, I told you. A spat.

HOLLOMAN
Really?

LAWRENCE
My life is not entirely a bed of roses, you know. It has its little ups and downs. Its ups and its downs.

HOLLOMAN
What on earth did you find to quarrel about?

LAWRENCE
Not quarrel. Spat.

HOLLOMAN
I thought you were madly in love with each other.

LAWRENCE
It was nothing. She accused me of cheating. She happened to be in my apartment when some woman phoned asking for me then hung up. All very suspicious. You know what females are like. Well, no. You don't.

HOLLOMAN
No.

LAWRENCE
Believe me—they are nothing like us.

HOLLOMAN
Really.

LAWRENCE
Let me illustrate. See this bag here. [*He blows it up*]
Watch this. [*He pops the bag*] See?

HOLLOMAN
Uh, huh.

LAWRENCE
A woman wouldn't do that.

HOLLOMAN
Why not?

LAWRENCE
Good question. It's the normal thing to do. But no.
A woman would've taken this and folded it up nice
and neat and put it in her purse. Don't ask me why,
this is one of those great holy mysteries of the universe.
All I know is, it's got something to do with saving things,
and wrapping things up, and putting things away in
purses. They accumulate things, Holloman. Things like
that phone call. You think she'll forget about that?
That phone call will be etched on her gravestone.
Because women, Holloman—women hang on to
everything. Forever.

HOLLOMAN
And you have no idea who she is?

LAWRENCE
My fiancée?

HOLLOMAN
The person who phoned.

LAWRENCE
I have my theories, yes.

HOLLOMAN
I suppose it could be one of the many other women.

LAWRENCE
Other women?

HOLLOMAN
In your life. There must be—

LAWRENCE
Right. Of course. You're right, Holloman—you're right.
As usual, you're—they'd be jealous, wouldn't they?

HOLLOMAN
It would be in their interests to really mess things up.

LAWRENCE
Sure. It would be in their interests, wouldn't it?
You're right. Absolutely.

Beat.

Why?

HOLLOMAN
To have you for themselves. That's obvious.

LAWRENCE

That's obvious, sure. And I'm flattered. I'm really—but still. Who?

HOLLOMAN

There are plenty of candidates. You've said so yourself.

LAWRENCE

Right. That what's-her-name in hosiery is always giving me the eye.

HOLLOMAN

That's a glass eye, actually.

LAWRENCE

Really? Well, she's certainly making the most of it. No. No, this is crazy, Holloman. I can't go around being suspicious of every woman I've ever slept with.

HOLLOMAN

Or haven't yet.

LAWRENCE

I know who it is. I know exactly who it is. It's the old girlfriend—

HOLLOMAN

Old girlfriend?

LAWRENCE

Why can't she just forget about me? Jesus. And that boyfriend of hers. Holloman.

HOLLOMAN

Psycho?

LAWRENCE
The guy has his name tattooed to the side of his head.

HOLLOMAN
That's handy.

LAWRENCE
When the fiancée answered, the old girlfriend hung up.
That's obviously what happened. I guess she needs me,
Holloman. But hey. I'm engaged to be married now.

HOLLOMAN
Right.

LAWRENCE
So we'll have to be very discreet. Is that a word?
It doesn't sound like a word. *Discreet?*

HOLLOMAN
You're planning on having sex with her?

LAWRENCE
Holloman, I'm kidding. How stupid do you think I am?

Beat.

Exactly. As much as I would like to help her out,
Holloman, I have my own future to consider.

HOLLOMAN
There's only one problem.

LAWRENCE
What's that?

HOLLOMAN
Now that suspicion has been planted in your fiancée's

mind, it'll be pretty hard to root it out. Won't it?

LAWRENCE
Uh, huh.

HOLLOMAN
But probably with your acumen, you already figured
that out.

LAWRENCE
I'll be honest with you. It doesn't work as well with
women. It's counteracted by their—you know.

HOLLOMAN
Intuition?

LAWRENCE
Is that it? Their intuition?

HOLLOMAN
You need a political way out of this.

LAWRENCE
Political. That's smart.

HOLLOMAN
You have to re-establish trust with her, immediately.

LAWRENCE
Right.

HOLLOMAN
You want her to believe you, don't you?

LAWRENCE
Of course. Otherwise I'll never be able to lie to her
for the rest of my life.

HOLLOMAN
Maybe you should just go to her, and confess.

LAWRENCE
To what?

HOLLOMAN
Your transgression.

LAWRENCE
My transgression. I like that. It almost sounds like
a good thing. *Transgression.* Wait a minute. Why would
I tell her I'm having an affair with someone that I'm
not even having an affair with?

HOLLOMAN
Sometimes a lie is just more believable than the truth.

LAWRENCE
Right.

HOLLOMAN
In her mind you're already having an affair, and that's
all that matters. It's pure strategy now.

LAWRENCE
Strategy. I like that.

HOLLOMAN
Think of it as plea-bargaining. You get off with the
lighter sentence.

LAWRENCE
Plus, if she forgives me, then I'm free to go ahead and
have the transgression.

HOLLOMAN
   Something like that.

LAWRENCE
   It's a crazy idea, Holloman. It's nuts. That's what makes
   it so brilliant.

HOLLOMAN
   No, you're right. It is nuts. What was I thinking?
   Don't do it.

LAWRENCE
   Hold on a second. What?

HOLLOMAN
   I've changed my mind. It'll only put your relationship
   in more jeopardy than it already is.

LAWRENCE
   You're such a neurotic, Holloman.

HOLLOMAN
   Am I?

LAWRENCE
   Jeopardy! Holloman! Jeopardy!

HOLLOMAN
   Are you eating the rest of that?

*LAWRENCE looks up a word in a little dictionary, as
HOLLOMAN eats his sandwich.*

4. The best laid plans

An outdoor cafe. LAWRENCE is wearing dark glasses.
HOLLOMAN returns with two coffees.

HOLLOMAN
O.K. I left a message.

LAWRENCE
Did you tell her all about how I turned over a new leaf?

HOLLOMAN
I didn't mention the vow of chastity part. I thought
maybe that was—sugar?

LAWRENCE
The wedding is only a month and a half away,
Holloman. A month. And a half. I want you to think
about that.

HOLLOMAN
And the invitations have all been sent, and everything.
And what about your *stag*?

LAWRENCE
That's happening, *irregardless.*

HOLLOMAN
It seems a little cavalier to be having second thoughts at
this point.

LAWRENCE
That's what it is, Holloman. You're right. It's cavalier.
It's completely...cavalier. Why isn't a woman more like
a—? You know.

HOLLOMAN
Man?

LAWRENCE
Holloman. Jesus.

Beat.

HOLLOMAN
Are you sure your car is O.K. where it's parked?

LAWRENCE
Why is everything such a worry with you? You're giving
me gas.

Beat.

HOLLOMAN
She needs more 'time' to think about things? What's
that supposed to mean. Don't you find that a little
oblique?

LAWRENCE
I'll tell you what I find it. I find it *totally* oblique.

HOLLOMAN
Why do people obfuscate like that? Why don't they just
come right out and say what they want to say.

LAWRENCE
No. They obfuscate.

HOLLOMAN
'Darling. I've met someone else.'

LAWRENCE
What?

HOLLOMAN
  I'm sorry. I shouldn't have said that. Oh, God.
  That was—that was—

LAWRENCE
  No. You should. Jesus. You should have said that.
  You're right. There might be someone else. How could
  there be? That's crazy. That's nuts. You're doing it to
  me again, Holloman. Look. You're infecting me with
  your paranoia. Jesus. Would you stop it? Stop it.

HOLLOMAN
  You're right. Who else could there be?

LAWRENCE
  I mean—

HOLLOMAN
  I mean, you don't want to brag, but look at you. Just—

LAWRENCE
  Well...I mean—

HOLLOMAN
  The envy of everyone. What you've accomplished.

LAWRENCE
  You're making me blush now, Holloman.

HOLLOMAN
  Salesman of the month.

LAWRENCE
  Please.

HOLLOMAN
  Two months in a row.

LAWRENCE
You're giving me a hard-on.

HOLLOMAN
Maybe even three months in a row. Who knows?

LAWRENCE
Actually, I don't think so. Not this month.

HOLLOMAN
No?

LAWRENCE
April. It's not really a suit-buying month.

HOLLOMAN
It's the cruelest month.

LAWRENCE
Besides, I couldn't really show up like this. Not for
a few days anyway.

HOLLOMAN
It's only a black eye.

LAWRENCE
All the same. It's part of my philosophy, Holloman.
I like to deal directly with the customer, as you know.
The sunglasses go against that philosophy altogether.
It might be different down in footwear. They might
have a whole way of doing things down there that I
don't know about.

HOLLOMAN
Or me.

LAWRENCE
But when you're selling a man a suit, there's a whole
relationship, there. Shoes, that's not a relationship.
An understanding, sure, but not a relationship.

HOLLOMAN
What about make-up? Have you thought about that?

LAWRENCE
Make-up?

HOLLOMAN
Around the eye? Just to cover the area?

LAWRENCE
I wouldn't be caught dead in make-up.

HOLLOMAN
And yet some people are.

Beat.

LAWRENCE
What did I tell you about that guy, Holloman?
Did I tell you?

HOLLOMAN
Will there be any permanent disfigurement?

LAWRENCE
What would make him think I'd write my old girlfriend
a love letter?

HOLLOMAN
What would make him tattoo his name to the side
of his head?

LAWRENCE
When was the last time I wrote anybody a letter?

HOLLOMAN
And how did he end up with it anyway?

LAWRENCE
Using words like *labidinous?* Just between you and me,
Holloman. I don't even know what part of the female
anatomy that is.

HOLLOMAN
Someone is definitely out to get you.

LAWRENCE
I never even liked her, you know. It was a mercy thing.

HOLLOMAN
And you're engaged to someone else, for God's sake.

LAWRENCE
Exactly.

HOLLOMAN
Well, technically no.

LAWRENCE
Not for the moment, no.

Beat.

HOLLOMAN
I think the transgression strategy might have backfired
a little.

LAWRENCE
You told me not to do it. You said it was crazy.

HOLLOMAN
    I said it was nuts.

LAWRENCE
    And you were right, as usual.

HOLLOMAN
    It was a dangerous plan.

LAWRENCE
    Give her time. She considers me a cheater, now, sure.
    But at least she considers me an honest one. Sooner or
    later, she'll come to her senses. I mean, Holloman.
    It's *me*. And I don't mean to—you know.

HOLLOMAN
    I know.

LAWRENCE
    But—

HOLLOMAN
    Exactly.

LAWRENCE
    Exactly. And the family loves me. Her mother finds me
    'enchanting.' You know what that means.

HOLLOMAN
    I worry, though. God.

LAWRENCE
    That's because you're such a worry-wort, Holloman.
    Things will turn out fine. They always do with me.
    Always.

Beat.

What exactly are you worried about?

HOLLOMAN
You've led a charmed life, that's for sure. But, I don't know. What if your luck is starting to turn?

LAWRENCE
Why would it?

HOLLOMAN
Was that your car?

LAWRENCE
Where?

HOLLOMAN
On the back of that tow truck?

They watch a car disappear.

Blackout.

5. When things start to go a bit off

An emergency room. LAWRENCE is a little green around the gills. HOLLOMAN wincing.

LAWRENCE
    What? What's wrong now?

HOLLOMAN
    The smell of hospitals.

LAWRENCE
    You are so sensitive, Holloman. I don't smell anything.

HOLLOMAN
    It's like a—cleansing smell. What is that?

LAWRENCE
    Cleanser?

HOLLOMAN
    Try and sit up straight.

LAWRENCE
    Why?

HOLLOMAN
    Because if you've been poisoned, you're not supposed
    to fall asleep. That's why.

LAWRENCE
    I haven't been poisoned. I don't even want to be here.
    I told you. I hate these places. I find them completely—
    antiseptic.

47

HOLLOMAN
    They're hospitals.

LAWRENCE
    I don't care. I don't think we should have them. I think
    the sick should just be sick and the dying should just
    fucking die. It's the old survival of the fittest, Holloman.
    You know about the survival of the fittest, don't you?
    Of course, when I look at you I think, Jesus, there goes
    that—I mean....

HOLLOMAN
    Right.

LAWRENCE
    Although. There are these fish parasites I heard about,
    once.

HOLLOMAN
    Uh, huh.

LAWRENCE
    They live off the backs of big fish by eating their
    dandruff. Basically.

HOLLOMAN
    Symbiosis.

LAWRENCE
    Is that what they're called?

HOLLOMAN
    Here. Take one of these.

LAWRENCE
    What is it?

HOLLOMAN
They're supposed to calm your stomach down.

LAWRENCE
I think I'm going to puke again.

HOLLOMAN
Yes. You should vomit. That's a good idea. You should stick your finger down your throat and you should go ahead and vomit as much as you can.

LAWRENCE
Actually, the word 'vomit' sort of makes you want to puke, doesn't it? Vomit. [*Extending*] Vomit. See?

HOLLOMAN
Yes. It does.

LAWRENCE
Look out, Holloman. I don't want to barf all over that nice suit of yours. That's a very nice suit.

HOLLOMAN
This?

LAWRENCE
Don't look so concerned all the time. It's a nice suit.

HOLLOMAN
Do I look concerned?

LAWRENCE
You always look concerned. You get those little wrinkles in your forehead. Those little wrinkles. Look at you. All worried. It's because you expect the worst to happen.

HOLLOMAN
It does.

LAWRENCE
I'll tell you a little secret, Holloman. It's my little secret, but I'll share it with you. Can I share it with you?

HOLLOMAN
Please.

LAWRENCE
Everything always turns out for the best.

HOLLOMAN
I think you've shared that with me before.

LAWRENCE
Example. My job. As you know, they reassigned me.

HOLLOMAN
They what?

LAWRENCE
Do you *ever* get any news down there?

HOLLOMAN
Where?

LAWRENCE
They've moved me over to ready-to-wear.

HOLLOMAN
How could they?

LAWRENCE
It's just for the time being. They got a complaint.

HOLLOMAN
About you?

LAWRENCE
Some little weasel in a big black moustache. I don't
remember any weasel in a moustache. Came in to
complain about me. Wish I'd been there. You know
what I would've done.

HOLLOMAN
Poured on the charm.

LAWRENCE
Poured on the charm, Holloman.

HOLLOMAN
This is unbelievable. Demoted.

LAWRENCE
Reassigned, please. But hey. That's the doggie dog
world of commission sales.

HOLLOMAN
Dog *eat* dog.

LAWRENCE
Eat? Dog *eat* dog? Holloman. Jesus.

HOLLOMAN
You were the salesman of the month.

LAWRENCE
Sure. You hustle. Some people don't like to be hustled.
They like to take their own pants off in their own time.
You know what I mean?

HOLLOMAN
Two months in a row.

LAWRENCE
Don't—remind me.

HOLLOMAN
This is—this is terrible.

LAWRENCE
Here's my philosophy on the matter. It was meant to be,
Holloman. The commissions are lower, now, so it makes
me work that much harder. Develop new strategies.
Complimenting people on cheap, shitty suits—for
example—that don't fit. That's a useful skill.

HOLLOMAN
Yes.

LAWRENCE
So you see, it's for the best. And the fiancée. She's not
speaking to me. Again. So what?

HOLLOMAN
But who would stuff their panties into your pocket?

LAWRENCE
Who wouldn't? Listen. It's for the best. The way I see it,
look—it's only intensifying our relationship. I've never
been hornier. I could screw that pop machine.

HOLLOMAN
Don't.

LAWRENCE
And as for my car. Well.

HOLLOMAN

How did it end up at the auto-wreckers?

LAWRENCE

It's just one of those things, Holloman. Somebody miscommunicates something, somewhere—a car gets demolished. You've got to understand that these things happen. For a reason. Although, even I'll admit that— what with my dog disappearing—it's been a tough week.

Wretches.

HOLLOMAN

I bet it was that sandwich. You know, I thought that place was a little suspect.

LAWRENCE

Look on the bright side.

HOLLOMAN

Of tainted liverwurst?

LAWRENCE

Look who I'm talking to. Mr. Negativity. When was the last time you had a positive thought? Hey Holloman. I want you to have a positive thought. Right now.

HOLLOMAN

Please.

LAWRENCE

For me. Come on. A positive thought.

HOLLOMAN

There.

Beat.

LAWRENCE
    That wasn't positive.

HOLLOMAN
    Yes it was.

LAWRENCE
    What was it about?

HOLLOMAN
    About? It was...about...I think it was about sunshine.

LAWRENCE
    No it wasn't.

HOLLOMAN
    It was. It was about sunshine.

LAWRENCE
    Were there any clouds, Holloman?

HOLLOMAN
    Maybe one or two.

LAWRENCE
    See? Even your thoughts have clouds in them.
    Even your thoughts. But then, who could blame you?
    No offence, but for one thing, you live with your
    mother.

HOLLOMAN
    She's in a home, actually.

LAWRENCE
    And they've got you down in the bargain basement,
    selling all those ugly discontinued styles.

HOLLOMAN
    Or—not.

LAWRENCE
    Is is any wonder you see the world the way you do?

HOLLOMAN
    No.

LAWRENCE
    Not me. No, sir. You know what I see? That nurse.
    I'm going to have sex with that nurse. You watch me.
    When her shift is over, she's coming back to my place
    for a light shagging. And tomorrow, I'm going to get
    up and go into work, and I'm going to sell a hundred
    and fifty cheap suits. After that, I'm going to take the
    fiancée out to a sad, romantic movie where somebody
    dies at the end. And when she looks over at me, I'm
    going to wipe a little tear from my eye. Because I am
    so goddam sensitive. And bang: we'll be back in
    business. And I'm going to do all this because I know
    I can. I'm positive.

HOLLOMAN
    Wow.

LAWRENCE
    Is it any wonder you admire me?

He starts to vomit as HOLLOMAN moves out of the way.

Blackout.

6. A conspiratorial air

*Seated together in LAWRENCE's apartment. LAWRENCE is
slightly shaken. He has a bandage on the right side of his head.*

HOLLOMAN

> You know, I'm beginning to get suspicious.

LAWRENCE

> For God's sake, Holloman. Have you never heard of
> faulty construction? It's called faulty construction.
> You think someone actually snuck in here and loosened
> the screws on the balcony rail?

HOLLOMAN

> It's a good thing I showed up. You couldn't have held
> on for much longer.

LAWRENCE

> And you thought my luck had run out, Holloman.

HOLLOMAN

> This is getting weird. And what about all the other stuff
> that's been happening? You have to admit it's—well,
> it's uncanny.

LAWRENCE

> Things fall on people's heads all the time.

HOLLOMAN

> On an escalator? In a department store? Table lamps
> don't just drop out of the sky.

LAWRENCE

> I wish you wouldn't talk like this. I just—

HOLLOMAN
    Alright.

LAWRENCE
    It gives me the creeps, frankly.

HOLLOMAN
    Fine.

Beat.

LAWRENCE
    And stop thinking about it.

HOLLOMAN
    I'm not.

Beat.

    So is that it, then? With her? Officially over?

LAWRENCE
    I tried to make it all look innocent. You know. How you
    do in those situations. But two naked people in a bed
    together. Even if one of them is a nurse. The medical
    angle didn't play with the fiancée at all.

HOLLOMAN
    No?

LAWRENCE
    God knows where I'll ever find another woman like
    that, Holloman.

LAWRENCE starts to cry a little.

HOLLOMAN
She meant a lot to you, didn't she?

LAWRENCE
Did I ever tell you how much?

HOLLOMAN
I think your colour is coming back a little.

LAWRENCE
I'll be fine. Do you have any more of those stomach pills?

HOLLOMAN
You can't take these every day.

LAWRENCE
Sure, sure. I know.

HOLLOMAN
Let's get out of this place.

LAWRENCE
I have to wait here. The police are coming by to ask me a few questions. And you know what they can be like.

HOLLOMAN
Police?

LAWRENCE
Didn't you know? Some money went missing from the cash in ready-to-wear.

HOLLOMAN
What's that got to do with you?

LAWRENCE
    I just moved over there.

HOLLOMAN
    And that makes you a suspect?

LAWRENCE
    Not a suspect, exactly. My position, for the moment,
    is under review.

HOLLOMAN
    You've been fired.

LAWRENCE
    No I haven't.

HOLLOMAN
    Yes you have.

LAWRENCE
    It's just until the whole thing is settled. Please.

HOLLOMAN
    This is outrageous. Don't talk to the police.
    You haven't done anything wrong. Have you?

LAWRENCE
    Holloman.

HOLLOMAN
    Right. Why should you be questioned?

LAWRENCE
    You're right. I don't have to talk to them.

HOLLOMAN
    Salesman of the month.

LAWRENCE
I showed them what a salesman was. I defined the
word salesman. I created an idea about salesman that
transcended all other notions of salesman. I took the
words sales and man and fused them together.

HOLLOMAN
On second thought, how will it look if you don't talk
to them?

LAWRENCE
You're right. I have to talk to them.

HOLLOMAN
Just don't be fooled by their line of questioning,
that's all.

LAWRENCE
Me?

HOLLOMAN
They'll get you to admit to something. It's the nature
of police work.

LAWRENCE
Don't worry. They won't.

HOLLOMAN
Won't what?

LAWRENCE
Get me to admit.

HOLLOMAN
What?

LAWRENCE
That I—that I—didn't—?

HOLLOMAN
You see?

LAWRENCE
Help me out here.

HOLLOMAN
Don't shake.

LAWRENCE
Right.

HOLLOMAN
You're shaking.

LAWRENCE
It's the accident. The accident.

HOLLOMAN
You're coming apart here. Don't sweat.

LAWRENCE
Am I? God. You're right.

HOLLOMAN
They notice that. They notice everything.

LAWRENCE
Then they'll notice that I'm innocent. Won't they?

HOLLOMAN
Of course. All you have to do is relax and pour on
the charm.

LAWRENCE
I'll just pour on the charm.

HOLLOMAN
No. Wait. It'll look too casual. You can't look casual.
You have to look innocent.

LAWRENCE
Innocent. Like this?

HOLLOMAN
Don't raise your eyebrows. That looks guilty. That looks
insane. Keep your eyebrows straight. Don't ever move
your eyebrows. And when you're trying to remember
something, look up to your right. I read somewhere—

LAWRENCE
Read somewhere! Jesus Holloman.

HOLLOMAN
If you're honestly trying to remember something,
you naturally look up to your right, whereas, if you
are only trying to pretend that you're remembering
something, you look up to your left. Or was it the
other way? No. It's the other way. The other way.

LAWRENCE
Left?

HOLLOMAN
Right.

LAWRENCE
I can't do this.

HOLLOMAN
You can do it. It's imperative that you do it. You need
to prove your innocence.

LAWRENCE
    My innocence. Exactly.

HOLLOMAN
    I know it. And you know it. But what do they know?

LAWRENCE
    Nothing, Holloman. They know nothing. What have
    I got to hide?

Beat.

HOLLOMAN
    You mean besides all that money you've got stashed in
    your fridge?

A curious look from LAWRENCE.

7. To better times

LAWRENCE and HOLLOMAN drinking beer. Some days later.

LAWRENCE
> Thanks again for getting me out of that—that—
> whatever they care to call that place.

HOLLOMAN
> Jail.

LAWRENCE
> I've never smoked so much marijauna.

HOLLOMAN
> I got you out but I didn't get you off. That's an
> appearance notice. You'll have to appear on that date.

LAWRENCE
> Right. Right.

HOLLOMAN
> Drink up.

LAWRENCE
> It's me that should be buying you a beer.

HOLLOMAN
> Sure. When you get back on your feet.

LAWRENCE
> Not just back on my feet, Holloman. Back up on the
> shoulders of other men. Because that's where I belong.
> I belong on the shoulders of other men.

HOLLOMAN
You know what most impresses me about you?
That you would think that.

LAWRENCE
Think it? I know it.

HOLLOMAN
That is, that is really impressive.

LAWRENCE
And all I need is a lift. A little lift back up there is all
I really need.

HOLLOMAN
Actually, right now, you need a lawyer.

LAWRENCE
Lawyer? What does a lawyer know that I don't?

HOLLOMAN
The law?

LAWRENCE
I'll argue my own defence. 'Your Honour...?!'

HOLLOMAN
Do you think that's wise?

LAWRENCE
Good old Holloman. Always the prudent one. I might
not know the first thing about the law. But I know this
much. I know this much, at least. I'm an innocent man,
wrongfully accused! I am a—I—I don't really have a
case, do I?

HOLLOMAN
No.

LAWRENCE
I have a couple of great-looking suits, though.

HOLLOMAN
Except that you—don't. Sorry.

LAWRENCE
Were they destroyed in the fire?

HOLLOMAN
Enough that you wouldn't really want to—wear them
again. Well, maybe to a costume party where everybody
had to...come as someone whose...apartment burned to
the ground.

LAWRENCE
Is there anything left?

HOLLOMAN
[*With slightly burnt suitcase*] I managed to—here.

LAWRENCE
Do they actually suspect arson?

HOLLOMAN
Apparently, they saw a man in a black moustache,
running from the building.

LAWRENCE
No kidding.

HOLLOMAN
It might be nothing, but I want you to come and stay
at my place.

LAWRENCE
  No.

HOLLOMAN
  I won't take no for an answer.

LAWRENCE
  No. No. *No.* What a weird word. 'No.'

HOLLOMAN
  Listen—

LAWRENCE
  It's a question of pride, Holloman. Try to understand
  that. I can't live with you and your mother.

HOLLOMAN
  I think someone's after you. That's my honest,
  heart-felt opinion on the matter. I think someone
  wants to destroy you.

LAWRENCE
  Me, Holloman? Me!?

HOLLOMAN
  Consider for a moment. Where did that money come
  from? And who put it in the fridge?

LAWRENCE
  I don't know. But I do know this. I should have kept
  my mouth shut.

HOLLOMAN
  It was the honest thing to do. It was the only thing to do.

LAWRENCE
  The police never would have looked in there.

HOLLOMAN
They might have. It isn't often a person inadvertently
uses the word 'refrigerator,' three times in a sentence.
Especially a sentence that has nothing whatsoever to do
with refrigerators.

LAWRENCE
It was the pressure of the situation, Holloman. I'm not
my usual self these days. Maybe I did steal the money.
What if I'm losing my—my—

HOLLOMAN
Mind?

LAWRENCE
You're right. You're absolutely right. I have to keep my
head about me, don't I? As bad as things are, they could
be a whole lot worse.

Beat.

HOLLOMAN
I'm trying to think how.

LAWRENCE
Right.

HOLLOMAN
Your place was torched.

LAWRENCE
I lost my job.

HOLLOMAN
You're a criminal, now.

LAWRENCE
An accused criminal. Let's not rush to judgement.

HOLLOMAN
Your fiancée dumped you.

LAWRENCE
In a manner of speaking.

HOLLOMAN
Your colleagues have all but deserted you. You nearly
fell five stories. Your dog was run over by a street
sweeper.

LAWRENCE
What?

HOLLOMAN
Oh. Sorry. Somebody called about the dog.

Pause.

LAWRENCE
You're right Holloman. As usual, you're absolutely
right. Things are pretty bad. But then, hold on a
second. Hold on there. Let's look at this another way.
You have to consider all the shitty things that *haven't*
happened to me.

Another beat. Satisfied, LAWRENCE goes off. Stops.

LAWRENCE
Hey, Holloman. I haven't been hit by a car, yet!

LAWRENCE smiles, exits whistling.

HOLLOMAN
　　No. You haven't.

HOLLOMAN, alone, sighs, takes his car keys out of his jacket pocket. Looks after LAWRENCE.

Fade to blackout. Music.

PART TWO

8. The welfare of his fellow man

Several days have passed. HOLLOMAN waits in a welfare office. LAWRENCE appears on crutches, in a leg cast, head completely bandaged, face partially covered in gauze.

HOLLOMAN
    I got your prescription.

LAWRENCE
    Look at you. How long have you been sitting here worrying about me?

HOLLOMAN
    Not long.

LAWRENCE
    You're so cute. You look just like your mother.

HOLLOMAN
    Whom you've never met.

LAWRENCE
    Aw. Haven't I?

HOLLOMAN
    Please.

LAWRENCE
    Give me the stuff.

HOLLOMAN
You could become addicted to this. This is very strong
medication.

LAWRENCE
What are you talking about? Of course it's strong.
It's a painkiller.

HOLLOMAN
If you want to take it, fine. But I don't think it always
helps you, because I think some of your pain is
emotional.

Beat.

That's all.

Beat.

LAWRENCE
Uh, huh. Is that right? And why, in your little worry-
wort mind, do you suppose they manufacture this stuff?
PAINKILLERS ARE FOR PAIN!! WHO CARES IF IT'S
EMOTIONAL??!!

HOLLOMAN
You're making a scene.

LAWRENCE
[*Calmly*] Say it. Painkillers are for pain.

HOLLOMAN
Painkillers are for pain.

LAWRENCE
Thank you.

Grabbing the prescription.

HOLLOMAN
  You've changed. You know that?

LAWRENCE
  [*Downing a dozen pills*] Really? How?

HOLLOMAN
  What happened in there? Did you sign on?

LAWRENCE
  Where?

HOLLOMAN
  They didn't turn you down, did they? They can't do
  that, you realize.

LAWRENCE
  That's not quite how it went. No. Actually, it went
  very—actually, it went better than expected.
  Actually, it was—

HOLLOMAN
  Why don't you just tell me what happened.

LAWRENCE
  Nothing. I walked in and I walked out again. Let's go.

HOLLOMAN
  What do you mean?

LAWRENCE
  I can't do this. O.K.?

HOLLOMAN
  You need money. You need a place to live.

LAWRENCE
　　And why do you think they invented credit?

HOLLOMAN
　　And how are you going to pay it back?

LAWRENCE
　　Debt is the backbone of this country, Holloman.
　　Besides, I have collateral.

HOLLOMAN
　　Right. Tell me again...?

LAWRENCE
　　My *future*—

HOLLOMAN
　　Your future—right.

LAWRENCE
　　My *future* is my collateral.

HOLLOMAN
　　Not without insurance.

LAWRENCE
　　I told you. I'm going to sue that guy.

HOLLOMAN
　　You mean the guy that got away?

LAWRENCE
　　I saw him.

HOLLOMAN
　　No you didn't.

LAWRENCE

I saw that big, black moustache of his.

HOLLOMAN

Really.

LAWRENCE

Anyway. To hell with it. I'm doing fine. I don't need money.

HOLLOMAN

Really.

LAWRENCE

I am boundless, Holloman. Look at me. Look.
I am unstoppable.

HOLLOMAN

I'm looking.

LAWRENCE

You're looking at the crutches, Holloman. You're not looking at me. Me. Look at me.

HOLLOMAN

Destitution doesn't suit you.

LAWRENCE

It's *welfare* and I don't believe in welfare. I believe everybody should work, or else they should fuck off back where they came from. Or else they should crawl into a hole somewhere, and disappear. That's the nature of capitalism, Holloman. That's the meat and that's the potatoes. And I love it. It's what I believe in. You know what else I believe in?

HOLLOMAN
    Yourself?

LAWRENCE
    Wrong! As usual you are wrong, Holloman. I believe
    in—Exactly! That's right. I believe in myself. This?
    This is nothing. You think this is something? This is
    temporary. The scars are healing quite nicely thank you
    very much, and I have almost no reaction to the steel
    plate, except that, lately, my head feels drawn towards
    the north pole.

HOLLOMAN
    I'd like to see you get through airport security with
    that head.

LAWRENCE
    And the cast comes off soon so I can start learning
    to walk again. Not only that—I have forty dollars in
    the bank. And a very nice parole officer. Have you
    seen her tits?

HOLLOMAN
    You're sleeping under a bridge.

LAWRENCE
    It's a hotel.

HOLLOMAN
    I don't care. It's under a bridge.

LAWRENCE
    You know what's wrong with you, Holloman?
    You have no faith in your own future.

HOLLOMAN
    Really.

LAWRENCE
    Really. You think like a bargain basement shoe-
    salesman, you know that? You've always thought like
    one. But then, holy smokes!! I guess that's because
    you are one.

HOLLOMAN
    Except that I'm not. Isn't that funny.

LAWRENCE
    Oh, you're not?

HOLLOMAN
    No.

LAWRENCE
    No?

HOLLOMAN
    I work upstairs. In the credit department. As a matter
    of fact.

LAWRENCE
    What are you talking about? No you don't. You do not
    work in the credit department. You do? No you *don't.*

HOLLOMAN
    But I do.

Beat.

LAWRENCE
    You've been—promoted? They—*promoted* you?

HOLLOMAN
    As a matter of fact, I—

LAWRENCE

Holloman, congratulations. I...Jesus. I.... Look at me.
I'm—what am I doing?—I'm shaking, I'm crying.
Look, Holloman. Not because I'm sad or jealous or—
I'm just so—I don't know what I am. I guess I'm moved,
Holloman. That a man like you, that a person of your
complete—pointlessness—could crawl his way out of
the oozing, primordial fluorescent swamp of the
bargain basement means that—well, I'm not sure what
it means. That in this world, it's possible for anything
to happen. That even though all your sad, little life
you've done nothing but peddle ugly vinyl shoes bound
with elastic bands—somehow, by some strange, perverse
twist of logic, stranger and more absurdly amazing
perhaps even than the formation of life on the planet
itself, you have found yourself delivered into the lap
of the credit department.

Pause.

I don't believe you.

HOLLOMAN

Fine.

LAWRENCE

When did this happen?

HOLLOMAN

I've always been there.

LAWRENCE

What do you mean? You—What? Why in heaven's
name, then, did you tell me you worked in footwear
of all places?

HOLLOMAN
I didn't.

LAWRENCE
You did.

HOLLOMAN
You decided that I worked there. When you befriended
me in the bar that night.

LAWRENCE
Bar? What night?

HOLLOMAN
You decided that I sold shoes, in the basement no less,
and that I lived with my mother. Which is fine by me,
except that it's not true. None of it. But that's fine.

LAWRENCE
Well, you live with your mother. I got that part....

HOLLOMAN
My mother is in a home. Like any reasonable son, I try
not to visit her. But fine. Think what you want to think.

LAWRENCE
'What I want to think?' Oh, I see. I get it. I haven't
been paying the slightest attention to you. Have I?
I HAVEN'T BEEN PAYING ANY ATTENTION TO
HOLLOMAN!!

HOLLOMAN
Pleeease. That's fine.

LAWRENCE
Is it?

HOLLOMAN
I've never been the kind of person people take much notice of.

LAWRENCE
Holloman, I feel terrible.

HOLLOMAN
Sure.

LAWRENCE
I *do*. I feel terrible. I'm going to pay more attention. To you. I am going to take an interest. In you. I am.

HOLLOMAN
I wish you wouldn't. I...really—I—

LAWRENCE
Tell me a little about yourself, Holloman.

Pause.

Come on. Tell me.

HOLLOMAN
This is—must we do this here?

LAWRENCE
Anything. What's your favourite colour?

HOLLOMAN
Really, I don't have a—I—I don't like colours. Particularly. But thanks for asking.

LAWRENCE
You don't like colours?

HOLLOMAN
No.

LAWRENCE
No?

HOLLOMAN
No.

Pause.

LAWRENCE
You see, Holloman. Here's your problem. You're
uncommitted. And do you know why you're
uncommitted? Because the minute you make a
decision, that's when you define yourself, and the
minute you define yourself—you stand to be challenged
by others. You're afraid to be challenged, Holloman.
Afraid to make your position known. Is that it?
Are you afraid? Are you actually going to spend the
rest of your sad, sorry little life, in the pursuit of
nothing but being a complete non-entity? No opinions,
no feelings, no attitudes about *anything whatsoever?*
Not even about a colour?! Because you're *afraid?*
It's just a colour for fuck's sake! A *colour!!*

HOLLOMAN
Periwinkle.

LAWRENCE
Peri—what? Sorry.

HOLLOMAN
It's a—sort of—dusty—blue—cornflower. Sort of.

Pause.

LAWRENCE

I want you to do yourself a favour. I want you to never mention that colour to anyone again. O.K.? If anyone, but me, ever found out that your favourite colour was *periwinkle*, Holloman? They would kill you in your sleep.

LAWRENCE hobbles off, shaking his head in disbelief. HOLLOMAN follows him with a look.

9. If seeing was believing

HOLLOMAN is leading LAWRENCE to a bench in the park.
LAWRENCE is wearing patches on both eyes, and limping badly.

LAWRENCE
I know what I'm doing. I know exactly what I'm doing.

HOLLOMAN
Do you? Good.

LAWRENCE
You know what that is? Instinct. It's instinct, Holloman.
Really. I'm telling you. Since the accident....

HOLLOMAN
Accident? Sulphuric acid?

LAWRENCE
Since the accident, I think my vision has improved.

HOLLOMAN
Well, that's one way of looking at it.

LAWRENCE
Definitely.

HOLLOMAN
Another way, of course, is that you're blind.

LAWRENCE
You know what I mean, though. My perception.
It's my perception I'm talking about. I sense things.
Is there a squirrel right there?

HOLLOMAN
No.

LAWRENCE
I thought I sensed a squirrel. Are you sure?

HOLLOMAN
No squirrel.

LAWRENCE
Are there any squirrel droppings? Look and see if there are any squirrel droppings, Holloman. Obviously what I'm sensing is that there was a squirrel there. Perhaps moments ago.

HOLLOMAN
I'm sitting down. Do you want to sit down?

LAWRENCE
No.

HOLLOMAN
Fine.

Sits, takes out a paper. Reads.

LAWRENCE
I know this place.

HOLLOMAN
We've come here before.

LAWRENCE
Hey. I think I can see trees over there.

HOLLOMAN
You mean over there where there aren't any trees?

LAWRENCE
My left cornea seems to be responding to the variations
in light.

HOLLOMAN
Really?

LAWRENCE wanders around a bit.

Don't wander off.

LAWRENCE
Good old Holloman. 'Don't wander off.' Like a mother
hen. I can just see you, standing there, right behind me,
watching my every step. Worrying.

HOLLOMAN
That's right.

LAWRENCE
That cute little forehead of yours all wrinkled up into
a tiny little, wrinkled up—forehead.

HOLLOMAN
Or not.

LAWRENCE
I think I'm actually walking better. Don't you? Look.

HOLLOMAN
If you say so.

LAWRENCE
People don't get gangrene anymore, Holloman.

HOLLOMAN
No. Not if their leg heals properly and they don't go

and sleep in a cardboard box in some abandoned railway car. I should have looked after you. I should have insisted. It's my fault. Damn it. You need to sign this—permission form—by the way.

LAWRENCE
Holloman. I've decided. I'm not going through with that procedure.

HOLLOMAN
I don't think you have a choice.

LAWRENCE
You understand me, don't you? My left leg is important to me. It would...it would be like losing—my right arm. Except lower, and on the other side. Last night I went over in my mind a list of all the parts of my body that were most important to me. Left leg was number four, for God's sake. It's the fourth most important part of my body, Holloman. I want you to think about that. That's pretty important. There's my right arm, there's my left arm. Then there's my right leg, of course.

HOLLOMAN
Of course.

LAWRENCE
And then my left. See?

HOLLOMAN
And what about your heart?

LAWRENCE
I wasn't counting internal organs. That's a whole different list.

HOLLOMAN
What about your head?

LAWRENCE
I forgot about my head. I guess that would be number
four.

HOLLOMAN
What about your penis?

LAWRENCE
My—? Jesus. How could I forget about that?

HOLLOMAN
A rearrangement of priorities?

LAWRENCE
You're kidding, right? You think I'm not interested
in sex anymore? I just have to find a woman who's
looking for my type.

HOLLOMAN
Yes, but where are we going to find a lobotomized—
hundred-year-old—troll—with an olfactory disorder?

LAWRENCE
The line-up starts here, ladies.

HOLLOMAN
They give you counselling afterwards, you know.
They do a whole grieving thing. You get to bury your
leg and everything. Have a little funeral for it.

LAWRENCE
I just don't want to be a gimp, Holloman. You see, the
thing is, gimps bug me.

HOLLOMAN
Lower your voice. There's a crippled—person over
there in a wheelchair.

LAWRENCE
Yeah? I can sort of make him out, you know.
He's in a wheelchair.

HOLLOMAN
Right.

LAWRENCE
Is it three o'clock?

HOLLOMAN
No.

LAWRENCE
Have you got my medication? Of course you do.

HOLLOMAN
Your credit didn't go through, by the way. You need
money to be a serious drug addict.

LAWRENCE
Did you try both my cards?

HOLLOMAN
They haven't worked for quite some time.

LAWRENCE
I think I have some air miles.

HOLLOMAN
Face it. You're destitute.

LAWRENCE
    I'm going to get a job, Holloman.

HOLLOMAN
    As what? A hat stand?

LAWRENCE
    Telephone sales.

HOLLOMAN
    If only you had a telephone. You know what?
    You can owe me.

LAWRENCE
    Holloman?

HOLLOMAN
    What?

LAWRENCE
    I owe you.

HOLLOMAN
    Right. I'm having some lunch. Do you want some
    lunch?

LAWRENCE
    Don't forget my medication is at three, Holloman.
    You'll tell me when it's three o'clock? Exactly?
    Holloman?

HOLLOMAN
    I might.

LAWRENCE
    You will. It's the one thing you've got going for you.
    Reliability. It's impossible for you *not* to tell me.

Your mind is like a—a steel trap.

HOLLOMAN
And your mind is like a sieve.

LAWRENCE
Wrong, Holloman. You know what my mind is like?
It's—My mind is like one of those—those—things with
the—holes in them. Everything passes through me now,
Holloman. Passes right through me. And why do you
figure that is?

HOLLOMAN
Fibre?

LAWRENCE
I am a conduit. A vessel.

HOLLOMAN
Oh, right. Egg salad or tuna?

LAWRENCE
I merely exist within this *temporal* framework, you see.
Details, such as are important to you, are irrelevant
to me, now.

HOLLOMAN
Good. Egg salad, then.

LAWRENCE
I want you to understand me, Holloman. You of all
people. Being the uptight individual that you are.
Would you like to know what I'm doing? It's kind of
a Zen Buddhist thing. Have you heard of that?

HOLLOMAN
Why is it always some eastern philosophy?

LAWRENCE
Eastern? It's from China.

HOLLOMAN
Why doesn't anybody ever become a—Lutheran?

LAWRENCE
You see, Holloman, what I'm doing is—I'm rising above this. Above these unfortunate—you know—these—

HOLLOMAN
—horrible...depressing...?

LAWRENCE
—predicaments, let's just say. I am rising above them. And I am allowing them to pass beneath me. I am lifting myself up and I am letting it all—

HOLLOMAN
Go?

LAWRENCE
That's right. Because it's not happening to me, personally, Holloman. It's just...happening. You see what I mean by perspective?

HOLLOMAN
I'm sure the drugs help.

LAWRENCE
I can do this without the drugs.

HOLLOMAN
Fine.

Pause.

LAWRENCE
What do you mean 'fine?' Holloman?

HOLLOMAN
Nothing.

LAWRENCE
Don't be *enigmatic* with me. I know you.

HOLLOMAN
No you don't.

LAWRENCE
I knew you from the first moment we met. I didn't
know the details, but I knew everything else.

HOLLOMAN
There is nothing else.

LAWRENCE
I knew you were the kind of person who was naturally
drawn towards strength and dynamism.

HOLLOMAN
Because I'm naturally weak. Is that it?

LAWRENCE
Something like that.

HOLLOMAN
So what about now? What draws me to you now?

LAWRENCE
Now?

HOLLOMAN
Now that you're sort of what ?—a helpless—deluded—

mound of unbathed and rotting flesh? I mean, aside
from that pigeon shit on your jacket. I guess it must be
your charisma.

LAWRENCE
It is. It is my charisma.

HOLLOMAN
Or maybe I really am a homosexual, and I'm secretly
in love with you.

LAWRENCE
I've considered that, you know. I have to admit, that
thought has gone through my mind.

HOLLOMAN
I mean—look at you.

LAWRENCE
It's the beauty within. It's the beauty and the dynamism
within that you find so irresistible.

HOLLOMAN
Is that what it is? I thought it was your staggering
arrogance.

LAWRENCE
Well that too, of course.

HOLLOMAN
I'll tell you one thing I find attractive. Very attractive
as a matter of fact.

LAWRENCE
My ass?

HOLLOMAN
    Your ex-fiancée.

LAWRENCE
    My—?

HOLLOMAN
    Oh, sorry. Didn't I—? Don't tell me I—forgot to—Jesus.
    Did I forget to tell you? I must have. We've been going
    out for some time.

Beat.

LAWRENCE
    What a—what a—cruel lie, Holloman. What a—what
    a—cruel, unbelievably horrible lie. You know as well as
    I do that if this was true, I'd go insane. The sheer irony
    of it would—derange my mind.

Beat.

HOLLOMAN
    You're right. I don't know why I said it. What a stupid,
    tasteless joke.

LAWRENCE
    You're damn right it's a joke. She wouldn't go out with
    you any more than she'd go out with a...steaming,
    roadside, *turd.*

HOLLOMAN
    I had you fooled though.

LAWRENCE
    For a minute you did. For a minute you had me fooled.

HOLLOMAN
> Gosh. I do hope you're not losing your sense of
> humour. That would be—really—that would be—sad.

LAWRENCE
> You are so funny. You think I'm—I'm—you think I'm
> losing my sense of humour? You make me laugh,
> Holloman. Hey Holloman, look. I am *laughing.*
> Haaaah!!!

HOLLOMAN
> Yes. I see.

LAWRENCE
> Ha, Ha, HA!!!

HOLLOMAN
> Yes!

LAWRENCE
> Ha, ha, ha, ha, *ha, HA, HAAAA*!!

HOLLOMAN
> Exactly.

LAWRENCE
> Exactly!

A beat. Blackout.

10a. A happy ending

LAWRENCE stands forward, crutchless, wearing bottle-thick glasses. HOLLOMAN stands upstage of him, to his right. It's too beautiful a day.

LAWRENCE
I told you I could do it. Did I tell you I could do it? What did I tell you?

HOLLOMAN
That you could do it?

LAWRENCE
And what did I do, Holloman?

HOLLOMAN
It's a miracle.

LAWRENCE
A miracle? Are you kidding me? This is—No, you're right. It is. It's a miracle. Actually, it's prodigious is what it is. *Prodigious.*

HOLLOMAN
I'm just amazed she took you back. Everything. It's...it's....

LAWRENCE
Why does the good in the world always take you by surprise, Holloman?

HOLLOMAN
Obviously marrying into a wealthy family can be very therapeutic.

LAWRENCE
What did I tell you about women and helplessness?
She took one look at that gangrene, and boing—arrow
straight through her little heart.

HOLLOMAN
How can you be so lucky? And the eye surgery.

LAWRENCE
Lucky? This is—you call this—? This is providence.
Do you know what that means, Holloman?

HOLLOMAN
I'm beginning to.

LAWRENCE
God is looking out for me, is what it means.

HOLLOMAN
I thought you didn't believe in God.

LAWRENCE
That doesn't mean He isn't out there, somewhere.

HOLLOMAN
What makes you so special, I wonder?

LAWRENCE
Huh?

HOLLOMAN
I mean, why should God, if He's out there, somewhere,
care about you any more than, say, a gazillion other
gangrenous, blind, self-absorbed, smelly people?

LAWRENCE
You should never doubt your own importance,

Holloman, even for a second.

HOLLOMAN
You doubted your own importance for a second?

LAWRENCE
I guess the words of the old song are true, aren't they?

Beat.

HOLLOMAN
Yes.

LAWRENCE
Suddenly, I've got this great big lump in my throat, Holloman. This—great big—this lump.

HOLLOMAN
I hope it's nothing serious.

LAWRENCE
Would you look at that. Just to see that sky again. You know what colour that is?

HOLLOMAN
Blue?

LAWRENCE
That's *blue*, HOLLOMAN. Not *periwinkle*. That's— that is *blue*. That is goddam—well, except for that big ugly grey—building...down there—that—

HOLLOMAN
Mental institution.

LAWRENCE
Really? You know, if those people could climb up here,

Holloman, I tell you. If they could see the world right now like I see it. Perspective is all you really need in this life. That's what happens to those people. In those kinds of places. They lose their perspective.

He studies the sky for a moment. A loud buzzer sounds.

LAWRENCE
Holy smokes. What was that?

HOLLOMAN
What?

LAWRENCE
That noise, Holloman. That weird—

HOLLOMAN
It's the breakfast bell. Time to wake up.

LAWRENCE
Wake up? But I—I'm—awake.

HOLLOMAN
They must have over-sedated you again.

Blackout.

10b. Meanwhile back at the asylum

A mental hospital. HOLLOMAN stands beside LAWRENCE, who sits in a wheelchair staring ahead. He wears dark glasses and is missing a leg.

HOLLOMAN
Some of these people seem quite nice. Mind you, they're insane.

LAWRENCE
Have you spoken to the doctor yet?

HOLLOMAN
No. Which one is it?

LAWRENCE
Do you see a woman over there wearing rubber gloves?

HOLLOMAN
That's a doctor?

LAWRENCE
No. But she thinks she is. Don't pay any attention to her unless you want a rectal exam. The doctor will be the only one around here wearing a belt.

HOLLOMAN
What'll I say?

LAWRENCE
Explain the mix-up. What else? How I was supposed to go to drug re-hab. How you accidentally took me to the wrong facility. Well, you know. The whole story.

HOLLOMAN
It's all my fault, isn't it?

LAWRENCE
Que sera, sera, Holloman. Just get me out of this.

HOLLOMAN
My stupid, stupid fault.

LAWRENCE
I just had the most beautiful dream, Holloman.
The most beautiful—prophetic is what it was. I could
see my whole future ahead of me. It was as bright as
the sky is blue.

HOLLOMAN
Lovely.

LAWRENCE
Holloman?

HOLLOMAN
Yes?

LAWRENCE
A question.

HOLLOMAN
Yes?

LAWRENCE
You didn't tell her I was in here, did you?

HOLLOMAN
I—might have mentioned...something. Why?

LAWRENCE
   I can't believe you're engaged to my ex. A woman of
   her calibre—I mean. She must've fallen on the soft
   part of her head.

Beat.

   Have you had sex with her?

HOLLOMAN
   I don't think we should discuss this.

Beat.

   That man over there has got a crayon in every orifice.

LAWRENCE
   Lunatics. Please.

HOLLOMAN
   You really mustn't look down on them so much, now
   that you're among them.

LAWRENCE
   I may be among them, Holloman, but I'll never be one
   of them. Despite the best efforts of this institution,
   I have remained in possession of all my—whatever
   they're called.

HOLLOMAN
   I know you have.

LAWRENCE
   What's that supposed to mean? 'I know you have?'

HOLLOMAN
   Nothing.

LAWRENCE
    You're very sly, aren't you, Holloman?

HOLLOMAN
    Am I?

LAWRENCE
    I can see what you're doing.

HOLLOMAN
    Can you?

LAWRENCE
    You're helping me keep my wits about me by being
    incredibly *obtruse.* You know as well as I do, that if I let
    my guard down, even for a minute, I'll succumb to this
    nightmare. So you're keeping me sharp. Grinding the
    edges of my mind against the wheel of your—the wheel
    of your—you know. Your—your—the wheel of your—
    what's the—the—I'm looking for just the right—

HOLLOMAN
    Malapropism?

LAWRENCE
    Tell me—when she talks about me, what does she say.
    How does she compare us?

HOLLOMAN
    She doesn't.

LAWRENCE
    I wonder if she thinks about me when she's having sex
    with you. I wonder if that's part of it. That must be part
    of it. What a game she's playing. Getting married to
    you, just to get back at me.

HOLLOMAN
You're becoming agitated. Should I take you back to your—?

LAWRENCE
Just—get me released, Holloman.

HOLLOMAN
You know, it's a lot easier talking your way into an asylum than talking your way out of one. Besides—what happens once you're free? You refuse to let anyone look after you.

LAWRENCE
The minute I can no longer take care myself, that's it. It's over.

HOLLOMAN
I wish you wouldn't talk like that.

Beat.

You have your whole life ahead of you.

Pause.

LAWRENCE cries.

HOLLOMAN
There, there.

LAWRENCE
Holloman! Why is this happening to me? There must be some reason.

HOLLOMAN
Must there?

LAWRENCE
    I've been thinking about this. I've been adding it all
    up, you know. I've been sitting here, adding it all up
    in my head.

HOLLOMAN
    And?

LAWRENCE
    I told the doctor about the little man in the black
    moustache. Although—I think that might have
    been a—

HOLLOMAN
    So now you believe there's a connection.

LAWRENCE
    You said yourself.

HOLLOMAN
    Did I?

LAWRENCE
    You saw him hiding in the rose garden the other day.

HOLLOMAN
    I saw *something* with a moustache.

LAWRENCE
    Why is he doing this?

HOLLOMAN
    Who knows. Maybe he doesn't like your style.

LAWRENCE
    Somebody drives their car into you because they don't
    like your *style?* Switches your eyedrops for sulphuric

acid? Burns down your apartment and kills your dog?!
That's *really* not liking your style.

HOLLOMAN
Hey—it's a crazy world. Sorry.

LAWRENCE
Whatever.

HOLLOMAN
People are killing each other in rush-hour traffic now.

LAWRENCE
That I can understand, Holloman. But this—this is—
what is this?

Beat.

HOLLOMAN
Total insanity?

LAWRENCE reflects, as HOLLOMAN considers him.

Blackout.

11. The penny drops

A forest. HOLLOMAN pushes LAWRENCE on a gurney. LAWRENCE holds a thick rope.

HOLLOMAN
Here.

LAWRENCE
Has it got a big, strong branch? It has to have a big, strong branch.

HOLLOMAN
Right.

LAWRENCE
Thank God I kept my sense of smell to the end, Holloman.

HOLLOMAN squirts a little "Pinewoods" air freshener.

To die, here, among the—

HOLLOMAN
Pinewoods.

LAWRENCE
Pinewoods.

HOLLOMAN
Right. This is where I leave you.

LAWRENCE
What?

HOLLOMAN
  I'm sorry. I can't be a part of this.

LAWRENCE
  What are you talking about? I can't see a thing,
  and I'm a complete vegetable. How the hell am I
  supposed to hang myself?

HOLLOMAN
  You still have the partial use of your right arm.

LAWRENCE
  Trying to brighten my spirits, Holloman?

HOLLOMAN
  Me?

LAWRENCE
  It's no use. I thought I could handle the blindness,
  you know. I thought, maybe, I could get by without a
  leg or two if I had to. I even thought I could live out
  the rest of my days next to a man who chirps like a
  brown nuthatch and eats marmite. But I cannot, I
  simply cannot any longer be the object of other
  people's kindness. Their pity. Especially yours.

HOLLOMAN
  Especially now. My God. I should never have left you
  at the edge of that cliff.

LAWRENCE
  How many times do I have to tell you? I felt someone
  push the wheelchair.

HOLLOMAN
  I know, but—

LAWRENCE
He thinks he has me cornered now.

HOLLOMAN
Luckily, you have one more move.

LAWRENCE
To finish myself off before he does.

HOLLOMAN
Very shrewd.

LAWRENCE
I can't take all the credit. You actually thought of it.

HOLLOMAN
Well. As a friend...

LAWRENCE
You have been a friend, haven't you? You've taken care
of me, Holloman.

HOLLOMAN
Yes. But if the only option left to you, now, is to live with
my constant doting—you—just—you—

LAWRENCE
I can't. Don't take it the wrong way, Holloman—

HOLLOMAN
No.

LAWRENCE
But I look at you...

HOLLOMAN
Or don't—

LAWRENCE
But consider you nevertheless, and have always
considered you my, well—my—what's the word I'm
looking for? Inferior? Well, you know what I mean.

HOLLOMAN
I think I do.

LAWRENCE
That doesn't sound right, does it? Not inferior—my—
my what, Holloman? My what?

HOLLOMAN
Protégé?

LAWRENCE
My protégé. That's exactly right. I've always considered
you my *protégé*, Holloman. So you see what I mean,
don't you? I can't have you feeding me and wiping
my ass. It's beneath me. And if what that specialist
told you is actually the case, and I really do have to
have a lung removed, I mean on top of everything else.
Why is it I have to have it removed again?

HOLLOMAN
Oh—some respiratory—

LAWRENCE
It doesn't matter. The point is—as you so correctly
observe—I'll have to be inside one of those giant—
whatevers—for the rest of my—

HOLLOMAN
Exactly.

LAWRENCE
But my mind will still be operating at its usual—

HOLLOMAN
Right.

LAWRENCE
Not only will I be in hell...

HOLLOMAN
You'll be painfully aware of the fact.

LAWRENCE
You and the ex-fiancée, stepping politely around my
iron lung. Your darling little children, tugging away
at the wires.

HOLLOMAN
Well, like I said. We could put you down in the
basement. In your own room.

LAWRENCE
He'll only come along again, with his big moustache
to perpetrate some new torture. I mean—he hasn't
'burned off my tongue with a soldering iron,' yet.
Has he?

HOLLOMAN
No. He hasn't 'plugged up your nostrils with fast drying
liquid cement.'

LAWRENCE
Who are we kidding, Holloman? Why don't we just
admit that I've had a run of bad luck lately. There is
no one out there. I know it and you know it. We've
been over this and over it.

HOLLOMAN
And over it again.

LAWRENCE

> And we're still no closer to the truth, because the truth is, it's completely illogical. Who devotes their entire life to destroying someone else's? What enemy could be so insanely devoted? *Who?*

HOLLOMAN

> You're right. It would have to be a friend.

LAWRENCE

> Don't be cryptic, Holloman. What do you mean?

HOLLOMAN

> Just that...you have to be pretty close to someone to hate them that much.

Pause.

LAWRENCE

> You're right Holloman. But who? I don't know anyone with a moustache.

HOLLOMAN

> It could be a disguise. Something to throw you off the trail.

LAWRENCE

> You're right, Holloman. Of course. It could be a disguise. Something to throw me completely off the trail. But then, why? Even a friend would have to have a reason.

HOLLOMAN

> Maybe they despise you.

LAWRENCE

> *They?* You think there's more than one?

HOLLOMAN
    They in the sense of he or she.

LAWRENCE
    I see. But if *they* despised me, then why would *they* be a
    friend?

HOLLOMAN
    Maybe they just pretended they were a friend. Maybe
    from the first moment they met you they decided that
    they wanted to destroy you. Maybe they didn't
    appreciate your smugness and your self-confidence.
    Maybe you represented to them everything that they
    weren't. Everything they could never be. But if they
    couldn't be it, then neither could you, you bastard.
    Or...something like that.

LAWRENCE
    You almost sound as if you know them, Holloman.

Beat.

    Holloman?

HOLLOMAN
    I do know them.

LAWRENCE
    You what?—you *know* them?

HOLLOMAN
    Oh for God's sake. *I am them.*

Beat.

    Since you asked.

113

LAWRENCE
You are not. You are? Why are you saying this?
What's got into you?

Beat.

HOLLOMAN
Do you—do you recall how we met? Probably not.
I saw you for the first time in the elevator that evening.

LAWRENCE
Elevator? What evening?

HOLLOMAN
You got on at the fifth floor. Remember?

LAWRENCE
This is all very specific, Holloman.

HOLLOMAN
Sorry. Little people dwell on little things. That's what
makes them so—little. It was closing time. I remember
what you were wearing. The polish on your shoes.
That hideous tune you were trying to whistle.

LAWRENCE
What tune?

HOLLOMAN
Exactly. How you waltzed into the elevator, looked at
the buttons, *and pressed 'G'!*

Beat.

   'G'!!

114

LAWRENCE
How else would I get to the ground floor?

HOLLOMAN
I already pressed it! I already pressed 'G'! That's how!!

LAWRENCE
Oh.

HOLLOMAN
But no. It was only by your pressing the button that
the elevator could possibly ever get to the ground floor.
My pressing wouldn't do it, you see. My pressing
wouldn't do it!! As if I needed to be reminded that
I didn't exist. That I wasn't even there.

LAWRENCE
Wait a minute. I thought you said you *were* there.

HOLLOMAN
I was. I was there! That's the point. No, that's not even
the point.

LAWRENCE
Jesus. You've lost me, Holloman.

HOLLOMAN
It didn't matter. I could have gone up and down all
evening. Up. Down. It's not like I was going anywhere.
I was probably thinking about killing myself, or
something. I bought a gun once, but I could never—I
couldn't—quite—It was the penny, though. The penny
that did it. That scuffed-up, that dirty little—
remember? No, of course not—that you bent down to
pick up off the elevator floor? As you pocketed that
filthy little coin, a little bell went off somewhere.
Well, actually it was...ladies' wear, but it coincided

115

perfectly with a thought I had. I thought to myself
"There's a man who's looking forward to tomorrow.
We can't have that, now, can we?"

Do you think it was an accident that I followed you into
the pub that night? Stood next to you, watching the
words gush out of your mouth like effluent pouring
into the river? Do you think it was a coincidence that
we became friends? Over a beer? Do you think I actually
drink beer? And what about the days that followed?
The complaints? The phone calls? The forged letters?

At first, of course, it was just good clean fun, but then
it became something else for me. Until I met you, you
see, I couldn't think of a single reason for living.
But then, wait! I forgot about revenge! [*Slapping on a
moustache with flourish*] See!? See?!

LAWRENCE
What? What?

HOLLOMAN
Oh, for heaven's sake. It's a moustache!!

LAWRENCE
A big black moustache?

HOLLOMAN
And when I hit you with my car, my God. I could—
hardly—*breathe* from the sheer hateful pleasure of it.
And then all the rest. The gangrene wasn't mine,
of course. That was just fantastic luck. But the insane
asylum was no accident. Or the fire. Or the acid.

Beat.

SORRY!

116

Pause.

LAWRENCE
Holloman.

HOLLOMAN
Yes?

LAWRENCE
I have to say this. I just have to say it.

HOLLOMAN
Go right ahead!

LAWRENCE
I love you, Holloman.

HOLLOMAN
You—? No you don't.

LAWRENCE
You really are a friend, aren't you? I mean—

HOLLOMAN
No.

LAWRENCE
To make up a story like that.

HOLLOMAN
Except that I didn't make it up.

LAWRENCE
To turn yourself into the bad guy. Into the villain of
the piece.

HOLLOMAN
I *am* the bad guy. I *am* the villain of the piece.

LAWRENCE
Just to make me feel like there's a reason shit happens.
That is beautiful. That is fucking beautiful. Thank you,
Holloman. Thank you.

Pause.

HOLLOMAN
But—

LAWRENCE
No, please. I know the real truth. But thank you anyway.
And I mean that. Because you know what you've done
for me, Holloman? You've cheered me up a little.

Beat.

HOLLOMAN
You're welcome.

Blackout.

12. Epilogue

HOLLOMAN's apartment. LAWRENCE in a large tub.
As he whistles, HOLLOMAN loads bullets into a gun,
awkwardly, alternately sipping scotch. LAWRENCE stops.

LAWRENCE
> Hear that, Holloman? I can still whistle. I can still
> whistle a happy tune.

HOLLOMAN
> Wonderful.

LAWRENCE
> You know what this is about, don't you. In the end?
> The moral of the story?

HOLLOMAN
> Retribution?

LAWRENCE
> We get what we get, Holloman. Exactly what we
> deserve.

HOLLOMAN
> And what did I do to deserve you?

LAWRENCE
> Are you kidding? You've been a loyal friend.
> Right there whenever anything went wrong.

HOLLOMAN
> True.

LAWRENCE
You know, I thought it would hurt my ego to have
someone like you take care of me. But actually,
in the end, I think it's bolstered my ego.

HOLLOMAN
Wow. Is that even possible?

LAWRENCE
Make sure to wash around my genitals, would you?
Use the rough sponge.

HOLLOMAN
[*Blandly*] By the way. I've decided.

Beat.

I'm going to end it all.

LAWRENCE
End it all?

HOLLOMAN
I realize, now, that in a life of useless endeavour,
vengeance, however pleasant, is merely a diversion.

LAWRENCE
Your life is hardly useless.

HOLLOMAN
No. You're right. There's a reason why I spend my days
trapped in an airless office cubicle, threatening poor
people over the phone with various forms of legal
action, then whiling away the dim, liquor-drenched
evenings trapped inside these peeling walls, washing
your nether-regions, while listening to another off-key
version of—Yellow Bird? What's the reason again?

120

Remind me. Oh, yes. Derision.

LAWRENCE
What about your marriage plans?

HOLLOMAN
I've never even met your ex-fiancée. I only said we were
engaged to completely and utterly demoralize you.

LAWRENCE
Good old Holloman.

HOLLOMAN
What do you think of that?

LAWRENCE
Still trying to spare my feelings? I can't believe I ever
thought so little of you, Holloman. That you were
always just a—sort of—what?—itchy hemorrhoid.
Well. You know what I—

HOLLOMAN
I know what you mean.

LAWRENCE
These last few days you've shown who you really are.
I owe my life to you.

HOLLOMAN
Life?

LAWRENCE
My life.

HOLLOMAN
You realize what you are, don't you? You're a blind,
one-legged paraplegic with no money.

LAWRENCE

But I'm a *lucky* blind, one-legged, paraplegic with no
money, because I have something very few people have.

HOLLOMAN

Let me guess. Faith?

LAWRENCE

Oh. I never thought of that. But you're absolutely right,
Holloman. As usual. I was going to say unlimited
personal appeal or something, but faith sounds so
much more—I don't know—high-minded. Yes.
I have faith, Holloman. In you.

HOLLOMAN

Great. Look. I'm going to blow my brains out. And—
and—it's up to you, really. You can sit here and rot
until you die, or I can accidentally drown you.

LAWRENCE

Are you being ironic again?

HOLLOMAN

I'm afraid not, no.

LAWRENCE

I can't believe—for one minute—that you would ever
leave me here, helpless, and on my own.

HOLLOMAN

Funny. I can.

LAWRENCE

After all we've been through? I know you better
than that.

Beat.

Good old Holloman. I can just see you, standing there.

HOLLOMAN studies the gun.

That worried look on your face.

Beat.

Holloman?

Longer pause.

You forgot to scrub my back.

LAWRENCE listens. Nothing.

You can't fool me. I know you, Holloman. I've always known you. And I'll prove it.

Beat.

Right. O.K. That's good. You're giving me a chance to prove it. Good. This is what I'm going to do. I'm going to let myself slip under this water, here. Just slip—under this water. You see what I'm doing? It's an exercise, Holloman. If you don't pull me up again, well—you understand what I'm getting at. The *preposition* that I'm facing you with. The only thing that can save me, now, is you. Understand? I'm putting my trust in you, Holloman. My trust. Because if I do that, I know you won't let me down.

Beat.

O.K. I'm pretty sure you won't let me down.

Beat.

Holloman?

*HOLLOMAN brings the gun to his head. A beat. LAWRENCE
slips quietly under the water. A considered moment. HOLLOMAN
continues to hold the gun to his head, resisting. He struggles until
the gun begins shaking. He looks at the gun shaking. Drops it and
looks down at the water.*

HOLLOMAN
Will nothing ever destroy you?! Nothing?!

He pulls LAWRENCE up by the hair. LAWRENCE gasping.

LAWRENCE
See!

HOLLOMAN
Before I kill myself, I just have to know. What makes you
such a fucking *optimist*?!

LAWRENCE
Good question. An optimist. That's a—it was my
father's dying wish, Holloman.

HOLLOMAN
Really.

LAWRENCE
No. But I thought it was. What he wanted was—he
actually wanted me to become an eye doctor.
By the time I realized the—you know—difference,
I'd developed quite the outlook on life.

HOLLOMAN
Why did I ask?

LAWRENCE
    I'd like to tell you a little story, Holloman. If I may.
    About life, et cetera.

HOLLOMAN
    Does it involve poultry?

LAWRENCE
    We had a neighbour who had this dog, once—this
    mongol I guess you would call it. This mutt. Always
    wagging his ugly little tail. Just so—happy this thing.
    The old guy could do anything to this dog. I'm telling
    you. Beat it. Starve it. Kick it down the stairs. It just kept
    wagging its tail. In the end, Holloman, what else could
    the guy do? He finally had to *pet* the stupid thing.
    You see? Persistence. That's the—the—

HOLLOMAN
    The—

LAWRENCE
    That's the *jest* of it, anyway.

HOLLOMAN
    The—*jest* of it?

LAWRENCE
    It means the essence, Holloman.

Beat.

    Holloman?

HOLLOMAN
    The jest of it. Right. I couldn't have said it better myself.
    Life really *is*—a joke.

125

LAWRENCE
 A—what?

HOLLOMAN
 Anything that starts and ends in diapers—I mean.
 That's—that's the jest of it.

He puts the gun down on a little table next to the tub, and looks at LAWRENCE for a moment.

LAWRENCE
 I don't...follow you.

HOLLOMAN
 No. You don't, do you? You really—you've somehow
 got it all figured out, but you haven't a—clue. You just
 blunder towards oblivion, ever the optometrist. Is that
 it? Of course. It's suddenly so obvious. Is it any wonder
 I missed it? Why are you happier than me? Because
 you're as dumb as a wooden *spoon*. I think too much.
 Is that it? That's it. I should just—live. Shouldn't I?
 I mean what else is there to do with my life? Besides
 end it, and it's too ridiculous to end it.

LAWRENCE
 [*With the gun*] Jesus. Is this what I think it is?

HOLLOMAN
 What else is there to do with my life? I'll tell you what.
 Absolutely nothing! Just—live!!

LAWRENCE pulls the trigger. A shot.

HOLLOMAN
 Or—not.

LAWRENCE
    Jesus!

For a moment, a strange stillness. HOLLOMAN has the look of quiet disbelief.

    What the hell are you doing with this? Jesus!
    I hate these goddam things.

HOLLOMAN slowly goes to his knees.

    Get this out of here before someone gets hurt.
    You're such a weirdo, Holloman.

Beat.

    And, about what you said, just now, about life, et cetera.
    You're right about a lot of things, Holloman, but not
    about that. Life is hardly a joke.

As HOLLOMAN'S head falls forward into the bath.

    On the contrary—*life*—I've come to realize, has a
    brilliant kind of logic. A brilliant and complex kind
    of logic. We may not understand the logic of it at times
    but that doesn't mean it doesn't—doesn't something—
    doesn't—what's the—what's the—word I'm looking for?

Beat.

    Holloman?

Pause.

    Holloman?

end.

Ideas for lion in Street

→ Point one what makes Laura so pissed)
- before groaning should there be a pause
- cut offs people need to keep talking and people need to be pissed
- Isobel

- "don't think this should be taken lightly" more pause afterwards

- unconcisonable
- period line needs to be more of a stab

- Rhonda needs to burst more after Coke addicts poisonus lines + Laura Needs to build more
- Rhonda Monologue